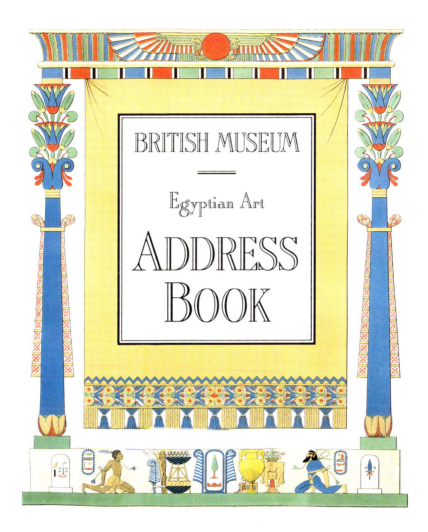

BRITISH MUSEUM

Egyptian Art

ADDRESS BOOK

First published in 1991 by Pavilion Productions Ltd
A division of Pavilion Books Ltd
196 Shaftesbury Avenue, London WC2H 8JL
Copyright © Pavilion Productions Ltd 1991
Illustrations © The British Museum 1991
Designed by Nigel Partridge
Typeset by PJD Photoset, High Wycombe, Bucks.
Printed and bound in Belgium by Brepols

ISBN 1 85145 617 1

All rights reserved. No part of this publication may be reproduced, stored in a retrieval system, or transmitted in any form or by any means, electronic, mechanical, photocopying, recording or otherwise, without permission in writing from the publisher.

Front cover illustration: The Pharaoh Sety I seated on an elaborate throne holding a sceptre. Before him on a table are stylized loaves of bread to sustain him in the afterlife. Watercolour copy by Henry Salt (c. 1818) from the tomb of Sety I at Thebes.

Back cover illustration: Three sons of Ramesses II in chariots at the Battle of Kadesh, copied from the Great Temple of Abu Simbel in Nubia. Engraving from J. F. Champollion's Monuments de l'Egypte et de la Nubie (1835-47).

Title page illustration: Papyrus and lotus columns supporting a winged sun disc cornice. Engraving from the frontispiece of J. F. Champollion's Monuments de l'Egypte et de la Nubie (1835-47).

INTRODUCTION

The British Museum houses the most extensive collection from Ancient Egypt outside that of Cairo. The mummies, which are undoubtedly the most popular exhibits in the entire museum, hold an eternal fascination for young and old alike. The artefacts range in date from 5000 BC to early Christian times, and include many types of object made from a variety of materials. There is one of the largest known collections of Ancient Egyptian documents on papyrus, and numerous stone inscriptions, wall paintings, metalwork, jewellery and textiles. There is a wealth of impressive sculpture, much of which is of colossal proportions. Many of the most important statues were acquired through Henry Salt (1780-1827) who was the British Consul in Egypt during the first part of the nineteenth century. Besides being a keen collector, Salt was also a skilled artist, and some of his finest watercolour copies of Egyptian paintings are published here in colour for the first time.

The first major study of Ancient Egyptian civilization was undertaken by a group of French scholars who accompanied Napoleon's Egyptian campaign in 1798. They took with them artists to record what they saw, and they eventually published a complete series of beautifully illustrated volumes on the subject. It was at this time that the French army discovered a stone tablet at a place called Rosetta. This was inscribed in classical Greek and two Egyptian scripts, hieroglyphic and demotic. After Napoleon's army surrendered to the British in Egypt, the Rosetta Stone was among the various antiquities handed over to them, and it has become the most famous single item in the British Museum. This inscription was to provide the French scholar, Jean-François Champollion (1790-1832), with the key to deciphering the elusive and mysterious hieroglyphic text. This was to take him some twenty years of dedicated study and earned him the title of 'father' of Egyptology.

Following this success, Champollion mounted a joint expedition with the Italian scholar Niccolo Francesco Ippolito Baldessare Rosellini (1800-43), to record the ancient monuments of Egypt in unprecedented detail. As a result they each produced a magnificently illustrated publication which did much to promote the study of Ancient Egypt throughout Europe. These detailed multi-volume works, together with the deciphering of the hieroglyphic script via the Rosetta Stone, mark the beginning of Egyptology as a separate subject. The British Museum's Egyptian Antiquities Department possesses an edition of these very rare volumes and some of the most visually attractive plates have been carefully reproduced exclusively for this publication.

These nineteenth-century colour engravings are still consulted by Egyptologists nowadays since they are often the earliest and most complete records of these

Geese feeding. Copy by Nina Davies (1936) from an Old Kingdom tomb at Maidum.

beautiful ancient wall paintings. Moreover, many of the ancient originals have been destroyed or have sadly deteriorated since their initial discovery, and some of the tombs which they decorate are completely inaccessible to most visitors to Egypt.

Another series of wall painting copies are also shown here, which are the work of Nina Davies (1881-1965). She was an excellent artist who went to great lengths to reproduce the ancient colours as exactly as possible in the days before colour photography. The remarkable accuracy she achieved with her careful work has enabled posterity to enjoy these precious and fragile paintings, some of which tragically no longer exist. Also featured here are a selection of the most attractive and exotic Ancient Egyptian motifs that have influenced and continue to inspire the decorative arts and architecture.

JAMES PUTNAM
Curator of Egyptian Antiquities, British Museum

The goddess Isis leads Queen Nefertari, wife of Ramesses II, to her tomb. Copy by Nina Davies (1936) from the tomb of Queen Nefertari at Thebes.

Name

Address

☎ Fax

Name

Address

☎ Fax

Name

Address

☎ Fax

Name

Address

☎ Fax

Name

Address

☎ Fax

Name

Address

☎ Fax

Name

Address

☎ Fax

Name

Address

☎ Fax

Name

Address

☎   Fax

Name

Address

☎   Fax

Name

Address

☎   Fax

Name

Address

☎   Fax

Name

Address

☎   Fax

Name

Address

☎   Fax

Name

Address

☎   Fax

Name

Address

☎   Fax

Name

Address

☎ Fax

Name

Address

☎ Fax

Name

Address

☎ Fax

Name

Address

☎ Fax

Name

Address

☎ Fax

Name

Address

☎ Fax

Name

Address

☎ Fax

Name

Address

☎ Fax

The Theban official Wahibre and his wife worship a group of gods in the afterlife. Watercolour copy by Alessandro Ricci (c. 1818) of a painted wooden stela found at Thebes and now in the British Museum.

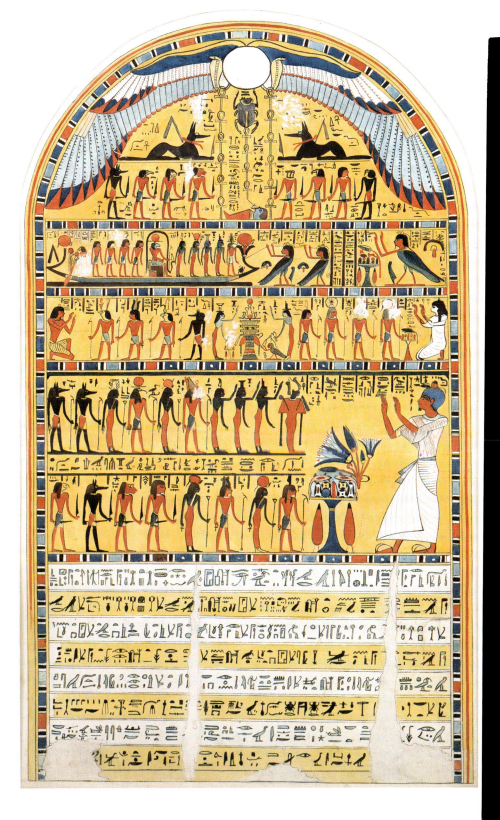

Name

Address

☎ Fax

Name

Address

☎ Fax

Name

Address

☎ Fax

Name

Address

☎ Fax

Name

Address

☎ Fax

Name

Address

☎ Fax

Name

Address

☎ Fax

Name

Address

☎   Fax

Name

Address

☎   Fax

Name

Address

☎   Fax

Name

Address

☎   Fax

Name

Address

☎   Fax

Name

Address

☎   Fax

Name

Address

☎   Fax

Name

Address

☎   Fax

Name

Address

☎   Fax

Name

Address

☎   Fax

Name

Address

☎   Fax

Name

Address

☎   Fax

Name

Address

☎   Fax

Name

Address

☎   Fax

Name

Address

☎   Fax

Name

Address

☎   Fax

Details of ornament from columns and central beadwork decoration (after Déscription de l'Egypt) from Décoration Egyptienne by Réné Grandjean.

C

Name

Address

☎ Fax

Name

Address

☎ Fax

Name

Address

☎ Fax

Name

Address

☎ Fax

Name

Address

☎ Fax

Name

Address

☎ Fax

Name

Address

☎ Fax

Name

Address

☎ Fax

Name

Address

☎   Fax

Name

Address

☎   Fax

Name

Address

☎   Fax

Name

Address

☎   Fax

Name

Address

☎   Fax

Name

Address

☎   Fax

Name

Address

☎   Fax

Name

Address

☎   Fax

Name

Address

☎   Fax

Name

Address

☎   Fax

Name

Address

☎   Fax

Name

Address

☎   Fax

Name

Address

☎   Fax

Name

Address

☎   Fax

Name

Address

☎   Fax

Name

Address

☎   Fax

An elaborate sailing boat, copied from a Theban wall-painting. Engraving from Niccolo Rosellini's I Monumenti dell'Egitto e della Nubia *(1832-44).*

D

Name

Address

☎   Fax

Name

Address

☎   Fax

Name

Address

☎   Fax

Name

Address

☎   Fax

Name

Address

☎   Fax

Name

Address

☎   Fax

Name

Address

☎   Fax

Name

Address

☎   Fax

Name

Address

☎   Fax

Name

Address

☎   Fax

Name

Address

☎   Fax

Name

Address

☎   Fax

Name

Address

☎   Fax

Name

Address

☎   Fax

Name

Address

☎   Fax

Name

Address

☎   Fax

Name

Address

☎   Fax

Name

Address

☎   Fax

Name

Address

☎   Fax

Name

Address

☎   Fax

Name

Address

☎   Fax

Name

Address

☎   Fax

Name

Address

☎   Fax

Name

Address

☎   Fax

Foreigners of Egypt beneath the royal throne. Copy by Nina Davies (1936) from a tomb of an unknown noble at Thebes.

E

Name

Address

☎ Fax

Name

Address

☎ Fax

Name

Address

☎ Fax

Name

Address

☎ Fax

Name

Address

☎ Fax

Name

Address

☎ Fax

Name

Address

☎ Fax

Name

Address

☎ Fax

Name

Address

☎   Fax

Name

Address

☎   Fax

Name

Address

☎   Fax

Name

Address

☎   Fax

Name

Address

☎   Fax

Name

Address

☎   Fax

Name

Address

☎   Fax

Name

Address

☎   Fax

Name

Address

☎ Fax

Name

Address

☎ Fax

Name

Address

☎ Fax

Name

Address

☎ Fax

Name

Address

☎ Fax

Name

Address

☎ Fax

Name

Address

☎ Fax

Name

Address

☎ Fax

The Pharaoh Tuthmosis I. Copy by Nina Davies (1936) from the temple of Queen Hatshepsut at Thebes.

F

Name

Address

☎   Fax

Name

Address

☎   Fax

Name

Address

☎   Fax

Name

Address

☎   Fax

Name

Address

☎   Fax

Name

Address

☎   Fax

Name

Address

☎   Fax

Name

Address

☎   Fax

Name

Address

☎   Fax

Name

Address

☎   Fax

Name

Address

☎   Fax

Name

Address

☎   Fax

Name

Address

☎   Fax

Name

Address

☎   Fax

Name

Address

☎   Fax

Name

Address

☎   Fax

Name

Address

☎ Fax

Name

Address

☎ Fax

Name

Address

☎ Fax

Name

Address

☎ Fax

Name

Address

☎ Fax

Name

Address

☎ Fax

Name

Address

☎ Fax

Name

Address

☎ Fax

The Pharaoh Sety I embraced by the ibis-headed god Thoth. Watercolour copy by Henry Salt (c. 1818) from the tomb of Sety I at Thebes.

G

Name

Address

☎   Fax

Name

Address

☎   Fax

Name

Address

☎   Fax

Name

Address

☎   Fax

Name

Address

☎   Fax

Name

Address

☎   Fax

Name

Address

☎   Fax

Name

Address

☎   Fax

Name

Address

☎　　　　　　　　　　Fax

Name

Address

☎　　　　　　　　　　Fax

Name

Address

☎　　　　　　　　　　Fax

Name

Address

☎　　　　　　　　　　Fax

Name

Address

☎　　　　　　　　　　Fax

Name

Address

☎　　　　　　　　　　Fax

Name

Address

☎　　　　　　　　　　Fax

Name

Address

☎   Fax

Name

Address

☎   Fax

Name

Address

☎   Fax

Name

Address

☎   Fax

Name

Address

☎   Fax

Name

Address

☎   Fax

Name

Address

☎   Fax

Name

Address

☎   Fax

Bouquets and arrangements of sacred lotus flowers. From Décoration Egyptienne by Réné Grandjean.

H

Name

Address

☎ Fax

Name

Address

☎ Fax

Name

Address

☎ Fax

Name

Address

☎ Fax

Name

Address

☎ Fax

Name

Address

☎ Fax

Name

Address

☎ Fax

Name

Address

☎ Fax

Name

Address

☎   Fax

Name

Address

☎   Fax

Name

Address

☎   Fax

Name

Address

☎   Fax

Name

Address

☎   Fax

Name

Address

☎   Fax

Name

Address

☎   Fax

Name

Address

☎   Fax

Name

Address

☎   Fax

Name

Address

☎   Fax

Name

Address

☎   Fax

Name

Address

☎   Fax

Name

Address

☎   Fax

Name

Address

☎   Fax

Name

Address

☎   Fax

Name

Address

☎   Fax

Female musicians at a banquet, copied from a Theban wall-painting now in the British Museum. Engraving from Niccolo Rosellini's I Monumenti dell'Egitto e della Nubia (1832-44).

M. C.

I

Name

Address

☎   Fax

Name

Address

☎   Fax

Name

Address

☎   Fax

Name

Address

☎   Fax

Name

Address

☎   Fax

Name

Address

☎   Fax

Name

Address

☎   Fax

Name

Address

☎   Fax

Name

Address

☎   Fax

Name

Address

☎   Fax

Name

Address

☎   Fax

Name

Address

☎   Fax

Name

Address

☎   Fax

Name

Address

☎   Fax

Name

Address

☎   Fax

Name

Address

☎   Fax

Name

Address

☎   Fax

Name

Address

☎   Fax

Name

Address

☎   Fax

Name

Address

☎   Fax

Name

Address

☎   Fax

Name

Address

☎   Fax

Name

Address

☎   Fax

Name

Address

☎   Fax

The falcon-headed god Horus, copied from the Island Temple of Philae. Engraving from J. F. Champollion's Monuments de l'Egypte et de la Nubie (1835-47).

Name

Address

☎   Fax

Name

Address

☎   Fax

Name

Address

☎   Fax

Name

Address

☎   Fax

Name

Address

☎   Fax

Name

Address

☎   Fax

Name

Address

☎   Fax

Name

Address

☎ Fax

Name

Address

☎ Fax

Name

Address

☎ Fax

Name

Address

☎ Fax

Name

Address

☎ Fax

Name

Address

☎ Fax

Name

Address

☎ Fax

Name

Address

☎ Fax

Name

Address

☎ Fax

Name

Address

☎ Fax

Name

Address

☎ Fax

Name

Address

☎ Fax

Name

Address

☎ Fax

Name

Address

☎ Fax

Name

Address

☎ Fax

Name

Address

☎ Fax

Singers, musicians and dancers at a banquet. Copy by Nina Davies (1936) from a Theban tomb painting now in the British Museum.

K

Name

Address

☎   Fax

Name

Address

☎   Fax

Name

Address

☎   Fax

Name

Address

☎   Fax

Name

Address

☎   Fax

Name

Address

☎   Fax

Name

Address

☎   Fax

Name

Address

☎   Fax

Name

Address

☎ Fax

Name

Address

☎ Fax

Name

Address

☎ Fax

Name

Address

☎ Fax

Name

Address

☎ Fax

Name

Address

☎ Fax

Name

Address

☎ Fax

Name

Address

☎ Fax

Name

Address

☎   Fax

Name

Address

☎   Fax

Name

Address

☎   Fax

Name

Address

☎   Fax

Name

Address

☎   Fax

Name

Address

☎   Fax

Name

Address

☎   Fax

Name

Address

☎   Fax

The Pharaoh Sety I clasps the hand of the goddess Hathor. Watercolour copy by Henry Salt (c. 1818) from the tomb of Sety I at Thebes.

L

Name

Address

☎ Fax

Name

Address

☎ Fax

Name

Address

☎ Fax

Name

Address

☎ Fax

Name

Address

☎ Fax

Name

Address

☎ Fax

Name

Address

☎ Fax

Name

Address

☎ Fax

Name

Address

☎   Fax

Name

Address

☎   Fax

Name

Address

☎   Fax

Name

Address

☎   Fax

Name

Address

☎   Fax

Name

Address

☎   Fax

Name

Address

☎   Fax

Name

Address

☎   Fax

Name

Address

☎   Fax

Name

Address

☎   Fax

Name

Address

☎   Fax

Name

Address

☎   Fax

Name

Address

☎   Fax

Name

Address

☎   Fax

Name

Address

☎   Fax

Name

Address

☎   Fax

The Theban priest of Amun and Osiris adores a group of gods in the afterlife, while above him is the sun god in his sacred boat. Watercolour copy by Alessandro Ricci (c. 1818) of a painted wooden stela found at Thebes.

M

Name

Address

☎ Fax

Name

Address

☎ Fax

Name

Address

☎ Fax

Name

Address

☎ Fax

Name

Address

☎ Fax

Name

Address

☎ Fax

Name

Address

☎ Fax

Name

Address

☎   Fax

Name

Address

☎   Fax

Name

Address

☎   Fax

Name

Address

☎   Fax

Name

Address

☎   Fax

Name

Address

☎   Fax

Name

Address

☎   Fax

Name

Address

☎   Fax

Name

Address

☎   Fax

Name

Address

☎   Fax

Name

Address

☎   Fax

Name

Address

☎   Fax

Name

Address

☎   Fax

Name

Address

☎   Fax

Name

Address

☎   Fax

Name

Address

☎   Fax

The sun god with his entourage travels through the night in his sacred boat. Watercolour copy by Henry Salt (c. 1818) from the tomb of Sety I at Thebes.

Name

Address

☎ Fax

Name

Address

☎ Fax

Name

Address

☎ Fax

Name

Address

☎ Fax

Name

Address

☎ Fax

Name

Address

☎ Fax

Name

Address

☎ Fax

Name

Address

☎ Fax

Name

Address

☎ Fax

Name

Address

☎ Fax

Name

Address

☎ Fax

Name

Address

☎ Fax

Name

Address

☎ Fax

Name

Address

☎ Fax

Name

Address

☎ Fax

Name

Address

☎ Fax

Name

Address

☎ Fax

Name

Address

☎ Fax

Name

Address

☎ Fax

Name

Address

☎ Fax

Name

Address

☎ Fax

Name

Address

☎ Fax

Name

Address

☎ Fax

Name

Address

☎ Fax

The lioness goddess Tefnut, copied from the Island Temple of Philae. Engraving from J. F. Champollion's Monuments de l'Egypte et de la Nubie *(1835-47).*

O

Name

Address

☎ Fax

Name

Address

☎ Fax

Name

Address

☎ Fax

Name

Address

☎ Fax

Name

Address

☎ Fax

Name

Address

☎ Fax

Name

Address

☎ Fax

Name

Address

☎ Fax

Name

Address

☎   Fax

Name

Address

☎   Fax

Name

Address

☎   Fax

Name

Address

☎   Fax

Name

Address

☎   Fax

Name

Address

☎   Fax

Name

Address

☎   Fax

Name

Address

☎   Fax

Name

Address

☎ Fax

Name

Address

☎ Fax

Name

Address

☎ Fax

Name

Address

☎ Fax

Name

Address

☎ Fax

Name

Address

☎ Fax

Name

Address

☎ Fax

Name

Address

☎ Fax

A ship under full sail. Copy by Nina Davies (1936) from a tomb at Giza.

Name

Address

☎ Fax

Name

Address

☎ Fax

Name

Address

☎ Fax

Name

Address

☎ Fax

Name

Address

☎ Fax

Name

Address

☎ Fax

Name

Address

☎ Fax

Name

Address

☎ Fax

Name

Address

☎ Fax

Name

Address

☎ Fax

Name

Address

☎ Fax

Name

Address

☎ Fax

Name

Address

☎ Fax

Name

Address

☎ Fax

Name

Address

☎ Fax

Name

Address

☎ Fax

Name

Address

☎ Fax

Name

Address

☎ Fax

Name

Address

☎ Fax

Name

Address

☎ Fax

Name

Address

☎ Fax

Name

Address

☎ Fax

Name

Address

☎ Fax

The Pharaoh Sety I with the god Horus. Watercolour copy by Henry Salt (c. 1818) from the tomb of Sety I at Thebes.

NAME

ADDRESS

☎   FAX

NAME

ADDRESS

☎   FAX

NAME

ADDRESS

☎   FAX

NAME

ADDRESS

☎   FAX

NAME

ADDRESS

☎   FAX

NAME

ADDRESS

☎   FAX

NAME

ADDRESS

☎   FAX

Name

Address

☎ Fax

Name

Address

☎ Fax

Name

Address

☎ Fax

Name

Address

☎ Fax

Name

Address

☎ Fax

Name

Address

☎ Fax

Name

Address

☎ Fax

Name

Address

☎ Fax

Name

Address

☎   Fax

Name

Address

☎   Fax

Name

Address

☎   Fax

Name

Address

☎   Fax

Name

Address

☎   Fax

Name

Address

☎   Fax

Name

Address

☎   Fax

Name

Address

☎   Fax

A procession of gods representing the provinces of Egypt, making offerings to the Pharoah. Copied from the temple of Ramesses III at Thebes. Engraving from Niccolo Rosellini's I Monumenti dell'Egitto e della Nubia (1832-44).

Name

Address

☎ Fax

Name

Address

☎ Fax

Name

Address

☎ Fax

Name

Address

☎ Fax

Name

Address

☎ Fax

Name

Address

☎ Fax

Name

Address

☎ Fax

Name

Address

☎ Fax

Name

Address

☎ Fax

Name

Address

☎ Fax

Name

Address

☎ Fax

Name

Address

☎ Fax

Name

Address

☎ Fax

Name

Address

☎ Fax

Name

Address

☎ Fax

Name

Address

☎ Fax

Name

Address

☎ Fax

Name

Address

☎ Fax

Name

Address

☎ Fax

Name

Address

☎ Fax

Name

Address

☎ Fax

Name

Address

☎ Fax

Name

Address

☎ Fax

Name

Address

☎ Fax

Finely worked gold vases and chalices, copied from various Theban tomb paintings. Engraving from Niccolo Rosellini's I Monumenti dell'Egitto e della Nubia (1832-44).

Name

Address

☎ Fax

Name

Address

☎ Fax

Name

Address

☎ Fax

Name

Address

☎ Fax

Name

Address

☎ Fax

Name

Address

☎ Fax

Name

Address

☎ Fax

Name

Address

☎ Fax

Name

Address

☎   Fax

Name

Address

☎   Fax

Name

Address

☎   Fax

Name

Address

☎   Fax

Name

Address

☎   Fax

Name

Address

☎   Fax

Name

Address

☎   Fax

Name

Address

☎   Fax

Name

Address

☎   Fax

Name

Address

☎   Fax

Name

Address

☎   Fax

Name

Address

☎   Fax

Name

Address

☎   Fax

Name

Address

☎   Fax

Name

Address

☎   Fax

Name

Address

☎   Fax

The Pharaoh Sety I before the god Osiris. Watercolour copy by Henry Salt (c. 1818) from the tomb of Sety I at Thebes.

Name

Address

☎ Fax

Name

Address

☎ Fax

Name

Address

☎ Fax

Name

Address

☎ Fax

Name

Address

☎ Fax

Name

Address

☎ Fax

Name

Address

☎ Fax

Name

Address

☎ Fax

Name

Address

☎　　　　　　　　　　　　Fax

Name

Address

☎　　　　　　　　　　　　Fax

Name

Address

☎　　　　　　　　　　　　Fax

Name

Address

☎　　　　　　　　　　　　Fax

Name

Address

☎　　　　　　　　　　　　Fax

Name

Address

☎　　　　　　　　　　　　Fax

Name

Address

☎　　　　　　　　　　　　Fax

Name

Address

☎　　　　　　　　　　　　Fax

NAME

ADDRESS

☎   FAX

NAME

ADDRESS

☎   FAX

NAME

ADDRESS

☎   FAX

NAME

ADDRESS

☎   FAX

NAME

ADDRESS

☎   FAX

NAME

ADDRESS

☎   FAX

NAME

ADDRESS

☎   FAX

NAME

ADDRESS

☎   FAX

A group of Nubian captives of Ramesses II, copied from the Great Temple of Abu Simbel in Nubia. Engraving from J. F. Champollion's Monuments de l'Egypte et de la Nubie *(1835-47).*

Name

Address

☎ Fax

Name

Address

☎ Fax

Name

Address

☎ Fax

Name

Address

☎ Fax

Name

Address

☎ Fax

Name

Address

☎ Fax

Name

Address

☎ Fax

Name

Address

☎ Fax

Name

Address

☎ Fax

Name

Address

☎ Fax

Name

Address

☎ Fax

Name

Address

☎ Fax

Name

Address

☎ Fax

Name

Address

☎ Fax

Name

Address

☎ Fax

Name

Address

☎ Fax

Name

Address

☎ Fax

Name

Address

☎ Fax

Name

Address

☎ Fax

Name

Address

☎ Fax

Name

Address

☎ Fax

Name

Address

☎ Fax

Name

Address

☎ Fax

The ram-headed god Knum-Ra, copied from the Island Temple of Philae. Engraving from J. F. Champollion's Monuments de l'Egypte et de la Nubie (1835-47).

V

Name

Address

☎ Fax

Name

Address

☎ Fax

Name

Address

☎ Fax

Name

Address

☎ Fax

Name

Address

☎ Fax

Name

Address

☎ Fax

Name

Address

☎ Fax

Name

Address

☎ Fax

Name

Address

☎ Fax

Name

Address

☎ Fax

Name

Address

☎ Fax

Name

Address

☎ Fax

Name

Address

☎ Fax

Name

Address

☎ Fax

Name

Address

☎ Fax

Name

Address

☎ Fax

Name

Address

☎ Fax

Name

Address

☎ Fax

Name

Address

☎ Fax

Name

Address

☎ Fax

Name

Address

☎ Fax

Name

Address

☎ Fax

Name

Address

☎ Fax

Name

Address

☎ Fax

The Pharaoh Tutankhamun hunting lions. Copy by Nina Davies (1936) from a painted box now in the Cairo Museum.

Name

Address

☎ Fax

Name

Address

☎ Fax

Name

Address

☎ Fax

Name

Address

☎ Fax

Name

Address

☎ Fax

Name

Address

☎ Fax

Name

Address

☎ Fax

Name

Address

☎ Fax

Name

Address

☎   Fax

Name

Address

☎   Fax

Name

Address

☎   Fax

Name

Address

☎   Fax

Name

Address

☎   Fax

Name

Address

☎   Fax

Name

Address

☎   Fax

Name

Address

☎   Fax

NAME

ADDRESS

☎ FAX

NAME

ADDRESS

☎ FAX

NAME

ADDRESS

☎ FAX

NAME

ADDRESS

☎ FAX

NAME

ADDRESS

☎ FAX

NAME

ADDRESS

☎ FAX

NAME

ADDRESS

☎ FAX

NAME

ADDRESS

☎ FAX

The Pharaoh Sety I embraced by the falcon-headed god Horus. Watercolour copy by Henry Salt (c. 1818) from the tomb of Sety I at Thebes.

Name

Address

☎ Fax

Name

Address

☎ Fax

Name

Address

☎ Fax

Name

Address

☎ Fax

Name

Address

☎ Fax

Name

Address

☎ Fax

Name

Address

☎ Fax

Name

Address

☎ Fax

Name

Address

☎ Fax

Name

Address

☎ Fax

Name

Address

☎ Fax

Name

Address

☎ Fax

Name

Address

☎ Fax

Name

Address

☎ Fax

Name

Address

☎ Fax

Name

Address

☎ Fax

Name

Address

☎ Fax

Name

Address

☎ Fax

Name

Address

☎ Fax

Name

Address

☎ Fax

Name

Address

☎ Fax

Name

Address

☎ Fax

Name

Address

☎ Fax

Name

Address

☎ Fax

Bath 8.92 : £3.99